100 Conditioning Workouts
FOR THE MODERN VIKING

by John Sheaffer aka Johnny Pain

ISBN: 0615683657

ISBN 13: 978-0615683652

Introduction

This book has been created out of a growing number of requests for "Greyskull Approved" conditioning drills. I have written and spoken at length about the trend in existence today for people to "condition for the sake of conditioning". I am a firm believer in having your conditioning work fit your individual goals. I believe that sports competitors are best suited by practicing their sport as their primary "conditioning". Strength training needs to form the base of any solid strength and conditioning program. It is going to have the biggest global effect on one's ability to perform well at a given task.

The workouts presented in this book are designed to accompany a solid strength-training program, not to take the place of one. That being said, these workouts are ones that I feel "make sense" for someone looking to get in all around better "shape" get their "wind up" and to use in conjunction with a well designed and implemented strength training program and diet to bring about a more favorable body composition, i.e. not be a lard ass.

Most would be well suited to apply my ten-minute rule to the workouts in this book. If the drill will take you longer than ten minutes to complete, then record what you are able to get done in that amount of time, and try to accomplish more on the next attempt (This obviously applies to those workouts that feature a set amount of work for you to get through). Once you can complete it all in ten minutes, then work on progressively bringing the time down. I want you to work very hard for a sustained period of time. One's ability to perform with the amount of intensity I like to see and have found to be necessary to bring about the types of progress that people want from their training begins to diminish rapidly after the ten-minute mark in my experience. This also brings up the age-old question of whether one would rather look like a sprinter or a marathon runner. Most will inevitably say they'd rather look like the sprinter (at least most who will read this book) however many still possess the antiquated belief that fat loss and conditioning both are best influenced by long, slow type efforts much more akin to the activities of the marathoner as opposed to the sprinter.

Each of these workouts is currently used or has been used in the past by members here at Greyskull and/or by consultation or coaching clients of mine training around the world. There isn't anything in this book that isn't suitable, in my opinion, for anyone looking to become more vikingesque and dramatically improve their pillaging game. They are not presented in any particular order, and I encourage you to use this book as a "recipe book" of sorts to help lay out your training. Plan ahead or pick one and go, doesn't matter to me. Just be sure you're keeping a good record to track your progress (progress is key) and that you are giving it your all and not leaving anything in the tank.

Good Luck.

#1 "13 Down" Kettlebell Swing/ Burpee Ladder

This is timeless classic. This workout has been used here at Greyskull as much as any other workout in this book.

It's very simple. Swing a moderately weighted Kettlebell 13 times and the immediately perform 13 burpees. Repeat this process with each number from 13 down to 1. Record your time and come back and smash it next time.

This works out to 91 repetitions of each movement. If you know going into it that this one is a bit out of your league at the moment duck the number down that you begin the ladder from.

Enjoy.

#2 The 100m Repeat

This one is very near and dear to me, and remains one of my favorites for both general conditioning, and as a high intensity tool to accelerate fat loss. It is very simple, head to the track, find the 100m marks, or just use the straightaway portion of the track if you're unsure about the markings. After warming up thoroughly, sprint the 100m as hard as possible. After you cross the line turn it around and walk or lightly jog back to the beginning. As soon as you hit the starting line turn it around and burn down the straightaway again. Repeat as many times as desired.

This one allows you to progress in two ways. The first is by building up the number of efforts. I normally will start people out with 5 or 6 and eventually work them up to 10. Additionally, you should be using your stopwatch to time each effort and give it everything you got to beat your time on successive sprints. It is normal for your time to increase a bit with each effort due to fatigue, but nut up and do everything you can to combat this. Dig deep and try to beat your previous time on each sprint.

When you can do 10 of these keeping your times within one second of each other with an honest all out effort on each, you'll be pretty badass, and I bet you'll be a bit happier with your body composition.

As a note, Florence Griffith-Joyner did the 100m in 10.49 in 1988, so be humbled and get after it trying to run down FloJo.

#3 Sandbag Shoulder and Squat x 50

We're going to enlist the help of our trusty sandbag for this one (details on constructing a Greyskull Approved sandbag can be found in Appendix A at the end of this book). It is simple. Start with the bag on the ground in front of you facing "perpendicular" to your feet (as shown below). Bend down and grasp the bag at by its sides, and hoist it up in a powerful motion to one shoulder. Once it has settled on the shoulder, execute a full squat. Stand completely, and bring the bag back down to touch the ground. No need to set it all the way down, just touch the ground and "shoulder" the bag to the opposite side before knocking out another squat. One shoulder and one squat equal one rep. Get through 50 of these as fast as you can.

The beastly will opt for the heavier (80lb) bag on this one.

Bony is one hell of a bag handler.

#4 10 Clapping Push-ups/ 40 yd Shuttle

Knock out ten clapping Pushups then sprint to a point 40 yds out and back, repeat.

This one can be done one of two ways. The first is to set a number of sets to complete and strive to beat your time each time you complete the workout. The second and perhaps nastier alternative is to work to time, meaning knock as many sets of this beast as you can get done in ten minutes. Either option will leave you gasping for air and hating life for some time.

This one is a bit more advanced due to the use of the clapping pushup. These aren't easy to perform until you can knock out quite a few pushups with ease (even then they are still a bitch). The obvious answer here is to use an alternative pushup such as a standard or feet elevated pushup to temper the difficulty a bit if this one is presently out of your league. It is also acceptable to begin with clapping pushups and switch to easier versions as you get into the latter sets (just be honest in your record keeping so you have accurate data).

Leave it all on the field on this one.

Continued on the next page…

#5 The Sandbag Half Mile

Here we're going to use our Sandbag we made again. This one is terribly simple. Cover one half mile on the road or track as fast as possible carrying the sandbag however you like. Run Forrest!

This is a gut check, the nutless need not apply. Set record, beat record, and repeat. Like I always say, this stuff is simple but not easy.

#6 200 Swings

This one has been a Greyskull staple for years now. Grab a Kettlebell (50lb or heavier for men, 35lb or heavier for women) or Dumbbell and perform 200 good swings as quickly as possible breaking as infrequently as you can. Work up to progressively heavier weights as you go.

Less than 10 minutes with a 70lb bell is a decent goal to shoot for.

Use your head here, I don't want this taking 30 minutes. If you are behind the curve a bit in the conditioning department start with a lighter bell or halve the number of swings. Keep it short; don't let it exceed 15 minutes or so.

For a really good time, do this one as a finisher after your deadlift workout.

Bony greatly prefers this grip on swings.

#7 The Sledgehammer Tabata

Get yourself a 10lb or Heavier Sledgehammer and a used tire. Swing the hammer and smash the tire as hard as possible as many times as you can in 20 seconds, rest 10 seconds, and repeat, switching hands each 20 second round. Complete 8 total rounds (4 minutes).

Score yourself based on the lowest number of swings on the tire you got during any of the 8 20 second rounds.

A score of 15 with a heavy hammer is pretty damn good.

Bony in rare form on the giving end of a Hammering.

#8 The Sandbag Clean and Press x 50

Clean your Sandbag from the ground to shoulder level and press it overhead 50 times as fast as possible. Duck the reps down on this one if you need to. Avoid the marathon session; if you can't rip through this one in a few minutes reduce the number of reps. Cap the session at 10 minutes and record whatever you have done at that point. Build up to fifty in less than 10 minutes and then work on bringing your time down.

Tommy the Sorta Rican Viking

#9 15 Tuck Jumps/ 15 Sit-ups x 10

Perform 15 tuck jumps followed immediately by 15 situps and repeat ten times.

This one has existed in many incarnations for sometime here at Greyskull, a total gut check. This is one of those great hotel room (or jail cell depending on your lifestyle) workouts that can be done in virtually no space just about anywhere.

Make sure you are getting your knees up high to your chest on the tuck jumps, most have a tendency to degenerate the movement to a mule kick-like hop sort of thing as time goes on and the suck really starts to set in.

The feet can be anchored on the situps if you wish, but it is not necessary. From experience, grass is the most forgiving surface to do high rep situps on.

Our ten-minute rule should be in effect on this one. If you can't complete it in that amount of time, do as many sets as you can, record it, and beat it on a later date.

Try to keep your lunch down on this one; those nutrients are necessary, hang on to them.

Bony could teach Buffalo Bill a thing or two about "the tuck".

#10 Dumbbell Snatch Max Reps in 10 minutes

Snatch a Dumbbell (50lb or heavier for a male, 25lb or heavier for a female) as many times as possible in 10 minutes switching hands as frequently as needed.

This one is modeled off of the famed Secret Service Snatch test. The SSST is completed using a kettlebell (53lb/m, 26lb/f) though, and we are using a dumbbell here. The reason for this is simplicity. The dumbbell snatch is an easier movement to perform from a technique standpoint. The kettlebell snatch can certainly be self taught, and I highly encourage learning the movement, however in my experience almost everyone can snatch a dumbbell with acceptable technique on the first try while the kettlebell version really challenges some early on. This combined with the nasty effects that high rep kettlebell snatches can have on the skin of the hands (we don't need blisters and tears jacking up our strength training progress or our Swayze style clay pot making) lead me to recommend the dumbbell version in this book.

Obviously if you are familiar and proficient with the KB version, have at it.

A passing score for the SSST is 200 snatches. See what you can do. Who's got 250?

The Dumbbell Snatch. Obvious puns being avoided here, I'm an artist.

#11 100yd Dash / Goal line Walking Lunges x 4

Hit the football field for this one. Begin at the sideline on the goal line and sprint to the opposite end zone. When you get there, turn, walking lunge to the opposite sideline and sprint back to the goal line where you began (this time up the opposite sideline). Do this four times, circling the field twice, and ending up back where you began.

Haul ass on this one. Establish a time and beat it. Add sets of two (one complete circle around the field) if desired once you are in stud territory, just keep it so that you don't have to slow down dramatically to finish the effort. You want to be blasting from start to finish on this one.

Make sure you're maintaining an upright torso on the walking lunges, and taking nice, long, even strides. Take your knee all the way to the ground (it's ok to touch it, it's a football field not blacktop). Don't cheat on these, do them right and make 'em count

#12 10 minutes- 30 Seconds On/Off: High Knees/ Sit-ups

Here's another great hotel room one that is quick and nasty. Set a clock to beep at 30 second intervals, or just watch your $5 stopwatch and alternate between high knees (running in place while pumping your knees high) and sit-ups, performing 30 seconds of each with no break in between, transition from one movement to the other as rapidly as possible.

Count your repetitions on the sit-up and try to maintain a decent level of consistency from minute to minute. A low number of 20 means you did pretty damn good.

Herschel Walker would be proud.

#13 50 Sandbag Burpees

These simple, evil ones are always my favorite.

Get your sandbag; place it on the ground in front of you. Get down on the bag as you would in a burpee, and bring it up with you on the way. Finish by pressing over your head. Repeat for a total of 50 reps. Your hands remain on the bag throughout the event after the first rep.

If you can't make 50 in the ten-minute window, record your reps and come back and beat them next time. Once you can hang, work on bringing down your time.

5 minutes on this one is pretty studly.

#14 400m dash, 75 Push-ups, 400m dash, 75 Sit-ups, 400m dash

This is a great one for the track or for your measured 200m turn around road point. Hit the 400m as fast as humanly possible then knockout 75 good pushups (no cheating reps) before blasting another 400. When you come in from that one, rep out 75 situps and then hit one last side stitch inducing, gut wrenching 400. This will take all but the most beastly individuals out past the 10-minute mark. That's ok. This is a good Spring/Summer Saturday morning one. If you can take the lack of variety for a bit, try dedicating 4 weeks of Saturdays to really improving your time on this one.

You will be happy with the results.

#15 50yd sprint/ 25 Tuck Jumps/ 50yd Bear Crawl x 6

Hit the football field for this one. Begin at the goal line and sprint like hell to the 50yd line. Once you are there bang out 25 tuck jumps, making sure you're bringing your knees up towards your chest as high as you can on each jump and not letting the movement degenerate into a hop with a slight mule kick. Once you're through the tuck jumps, get down and bear crawl it the rest of the way to the opposite goal line from where you started. Turn around and repeat for a total of six trips downfield.

This one is fun and has a grade school gym class feel to it. Enjoy the variety.

This is another one that will push many out past 10 minutes if you're not a stud yet. That's fine. Dedicate some time to bringing down your time if need be. Remember, any of these can be done for several workouts in a row. Setting a goal and sticking to it is always a good idea.

#16 5 Push-ups, 5 Hanging Leg Raise Max Sets in 7 minutes

You'll need a pull up bar that you can jump and grab on this one. Start your stopwatch or set a countdown timer for ten minutes. Bust out five solid pushups and then hit the pull up bar. Pause to make your body still if need be (no swinging) and bring your knees high up into your chest. Drop down from the bar and repeat the process. That completes one set. Knock out as many sets as you can in 7 minutes.

More advanced individuals might keep their legs extended on the leg raise portion or even bring their toes up to touch the bar which puts another evil and exciting spin on things. This is not about speed at the expense of quality movements. Make sure you're not wildly swinging on the bar and that you're doing a smooth knee or leg raise on each repetition.

#17 10 Bodyweight Squats, 2 Greyskull Grinders Max sets in 10 minutes

For this one you will need a pull up bar. Here we will use two movements, a simple unloaded, bodyweight squat, and the devastating Greyskull favorite the Grinder. Start your stopwatch or set a countdown timer for ten minutes and bust out ten good bodyweight squats, making sure to get proper depth on each (hips below knees), then jump to the pull up bar and bust out two grinders. The grinder is performed by executing a basic chin up, returning to the bottom, dead hang position, and then excuting a hanging knee or leg raise. Make both movements distinct and high quality. Flailing or swinging the reps is unacceptable. This is a gut buster. Tough it out and set a record to beat later.

#18 (Barbell Hang Power Clean + Push Press x 3) 5x5

Load a barbell with a moderate weight. Remember we aren't trying to strength train here, so make sure the loads used will allow you to complete all of the reps of each set without needing to set the bar down (though I should add that this certainly should not be an easy weight). Add weight gradually once the criteria is met and times improve over a series of workouts.

Begin with the barbell in the "hang" position. Power Clean the bar to your shoulders and then perform 3 push presses. That completes one rep. Return the bar to the hang position for the start of the second rep. 5 reps makes one set. We're doing 5 sets here.

Rest one minute in between sets. Score yourself based on the time it takes to complete your slowest set.

#19 Barbell Hang Power Snatch x 2 + Overhead Lunge L/R x 5 x 5

Begin with a barbell in the hang position. Perform a power snatch and return the bar to the hang position. From there execute a second power snatch and then leave the bar overhead. With the bar supported overhead, perform a lunge step forward with the left leg, return it, and then perform a lunge step forward with the right leg. That completes one repetition of the complex. Bust out five reps before setting the bar down.

Time yourself on each set and rest one minute in between sets.

Pick a manageable weight that will let you perform an uninterrupted set of five of this complex. This might take a little playing around to get right the first time. Like all barbell complexes, we aim to very slowly increase the weight used as well as bring down the time it takes to complete the workout.

#20 40 Burpee Grinders

Grueling and nasty is the only way to describe this one. Work it down to an impressive time and you will surely be a beast.

As the name suggests, this is simply a combination Burpee/ Greyskull Grinder. Complete a burpee, but jump and catch the pull up bar at the top of the movement. Make your body still in the dead hang position and then execute a chin-up. Return to the bottom, dead hang position, and then raise your knees (or your extended legs if you dare) as high as you can. That's one.

Do forty of these as fast as possible without sacrificing quality for speed.

Continued on next page…

#21 5 Burpees/ 10 Push-ups x 10

Quick, simple, and to the point, this one is often used here as a finisher and is used by many as a "get it in" type of thing when time is short and they want a fast, effective, stimulus for the day.

Do five burpees then ten pushups (one set) ten times. Record your time and call it a day.

Duck down the number of sets if need be. This one shouldn't be a long, painful bastard. Short and nasty is the word here.

#22 Road Mile Stop Sign Run

Suburbanites take notice, this one's for you.

This one is a simple and timeless old favorite here. This was one of the more common workouts done here in the very early days of Greyskull.

Scout out a one-mile course on the road through a neighborhood if geography allows. Run the course as fast as possible stopping at each stop sign to perform five of one of the following exercises:

-Bodyweight Squat
-Push-up
-Burpee

Only do one exercise per stop sign and rotate through them as you go. The order isn't important, just keep cycling through them as you run.

Run the same course each time and time the entire thing. Philadelphia winters make this one especially fun.

#23 Broad Jump Burpee/ Dumbbell Hang Clean and Press 5 x 6/6

Perform a burpee and then execute a forward leap as far as possible during the jump portion. Turn and face the direction you started and repeat the process from the beginning, leaving you back at the same point you began. Each jump marks the end of one repetition. Complete six repetitions and then grab hold of two heavy dumbbells (don't be a pussy on these). Clean the dumbbells to your shoulders and then press them overhead. That is one repetition. Return the Dumbbells to the hang position and knock out five more for a total of six repetitions. Six and Six equals one set. Rip through five of these as fast as you can.

I used to do these a lot with my clients and would put a nasty spin on things. At the beginning of the session I would ask them to broad jump for me. I would then mark the point to which they jumped, normally after they tried three or four times to get as far as possible (gotta love the competitive nature of people). I would purposely mark their landing point a few inches short of where they had actually landed. This would be met with serious resistance and they would insist that they had jumped farther. I would say "Ok" and then replace the mark to where they indicated. After this process was complete I would fill them in on what they would be doing and then let them know that any rep that they did not jump past their mark did not count.

Man did they dislike me for that. Kept them honest though. Try it. No need to trick yourself, just make a line to cross with your jumps and hold yourself accountable for the distance.

Continued on next page...

#24 Tabata Front Squat

This one I have to attribute to Dan John. This was my first introduction to the Tabata method several years ago, and remains one of my favorite short, intense conditioning workouts and also, in my opinion, one of the nastiest activities a human can put themselves through.

It is incredibly simple; clean a barbell to your shoulders to the "rack position". Start a clock or set an interval timer to beep Tabata style (at 20 second/ 10 second intervals). Front Squat the barbell as many times as you can in the 20 seconds and then rest (still holding the bar) for 10 seconds. The effectiveness of this one decreases, in my opinion, if you attempt to use too heavy of a weight. I would not recommend exceeding 65-75lbs no matter how much of a badass you are.

As with any Tabata, your score is the lowest number of repetitions you complete during any of the eight 20 second periods.

After you complete this one, curse Dan John and then drop him a thank you.

#25 Barbell Waiter's Walk Half Mile

This one will give you a newfound understanding of the function of your abdominal muscles in stabilizing a load overhead. It will also help develop tremendous strength and stability in the whole shoulder girdle. I have long been a big fan of the Waiter's Walk.

Execution is straightforward, pick up a barbell, press it overhead, and cover one half mile as rapidly as possible.

The trick here is selecting a weight that challenges you, yet is not so heavy that holding the bar overhead becomes a more difficult task then traversing the distance. If you have to stop frequently to set down the bar, you are using too much weight. Fast and nasty is the rule here.

Enjoy the sore abs you'll get from this one. Be prepared if you've never done this before.

#26 Dumbbell Squat/ Press/ Squat and Press x 5/5/5 Max Sets in 7 minutes

An old favorite; Begin with two moderately weighted dumbbells held at your shoulders as if you were going to press them. Start a 7 minute clock and perform 5 squats holding the bells, followed by 5 presses (a push is OK), followed by 5 Squat and Presses (what some will call "Thrusters") as many times as possible before time runs out.

Don't go too heavy on the dumbbells here, this is conditioning, not strength training. If you need to set the bells down frequently, or have difficulty getting them locked out over your head on any of the reps then you need to reduce the weight.

This is just awful.

#27 50 "Manmakers"

There are many different incarnations of this dumbbell complex. The version described below is the version we've used at Greyskull for several years now.

The Manmaker is performed by holding two dumbbells in your hands, placing them on the ground in front of you, assuming a "plank" or pushup position with your hands on the bells, rowing the left bell up along side your chest while keeping your body from twisting excessively, returning the bell, executing a pushup, rowing the right bell, returning it, then jumping your feet up between the bells as in the burpee, and lastly, "cleaning" the bells to your shoulders and performing a press.

This one is tough to beat as a total body smoker of a conditioning tool. Keep the weights light, I wouldn't suggest more than 35lbs for even the toughest of tough guys.

Rip through 50 of these bad boys as fast as possible. As with other drills in this book, if you cannot complete all 50 in less than 10 minutes, record the number of repetitions you have completed and then beat that number next time. Once you break the ten-minute mark, work on bringing down your time.

The "Manmaker", continued on next page...

#28 25 Dumbbell Overhead Walking Lunge/ 25 Tuck Jumps x 4

Awful. Bony used to lose it on this one every time.

Quick story: once he and I did this one in the original backyard Greyskull. In true Bony fashion he began heaving about 3 sets into it. While heaving he noticed that he had stepped in dog shit, at which point his heaving became more intense. Again, in true Bony fashion, he removed his shoe and began hopping on his other foot (still retching) only to lose his balance and set his foot (the one now only in a sock) down in the very same dog shit he had stepped in with his shoe on.

Hold a heavy dumbbell (or kettlebell) overhead with one arm. Complete 25 walking lunge steps, counting each step as one, set the dumbbell down, and bust out 25 good tuck jumps. Bring your knees high to your chest on each rep and stay as upright as possible. Pick up the dumbbell in the hand opposite the one you used for the first set and do the same. Switch hands two more times for a total of 4 sets.

Simple, not easy.

#29 (Dumbbell Push-up/ Row x 10, Dumbbell Overhead Sit-up x 10) x 5

Great Dumbbell Workout here. Pick a pair of bells that represent a challenge but aren't too heavy for this one. I wouldn't exceed about 40lbs even for the super studs.

Assume the pushup position holding the bells in your hands. Execute a pushup and then row the left dumbbell up alongside your chest without twisting your body to the side. Twisting is fruity, don't do it. That counts as one repetition. With the bell back on the ground, perform another pushup and then row with the opposite arm. Two down. Continue out a set of ten. When you have completed ten pushup/ rows, assume a sit-up position with the bells held out over your chest, arms extended, as if you were about to do a floor press. Sit-up, allowing your arms to travel as needed in order to keep the bells locked out. In the top position of the sit-up, your arms will be extended over your head as if you just completed a dumbbell press. Knock out 10 of those to finish one set of the complex.

Take down 5 sets of this killer and call it a day. Come back and beat your time another day.

Continued on next page…

#30 (Burpee x 20 / 50 yd Shuttle) x 4

Back to the football field for this one. Stand on the goal line and knock out 20 burpees as fast as possible. When you've hit 20, sprint like hell out to the 50 yd line and back. Repeat 3 more times for a total of 4 sets.

Less than 5 minutes is damn good.

#31 400m Sprint, 100 KB Swings, 400m Sprint

Pretty Straightforward, hit the track or measure out a 400m course on the road. Sprint the 400m, immediately pick up the Kettlebell (or Dumbbell) and perform 100 swings, then it's back to the track or course for one last hard 400m. Record your time for the day and beat it on the next effort.

Get it done and call it a day. This one is nasty.

#32 Sandbag Get-up x 30

Bring out the bag for this one.

Lie down on your back and place the bag on your chest, favoring one side (as shown). While holding the bag as if you'd just "shouldered" it, get up to your feet. Once you are standing, reverse the process and head back down to the supine position. While on the ground switch sides with the bag and complete the process. Alternate sides on each repetition for a total of 30 reps.

Blaze through this one, record your time, and call it a day.

Studs, use the heavy bag or tack on an additional 10 or 20 reps.

#33 5 Gladiator Push-up / 5 Dumbbell Burpee x 10

This one will require two dumbbells on the fairly heavy side. The Gladiator Pushup will be the weak link, so use a weight that allows you to complete the required reps of that exercise but presents a pretty significant challenge. We don't want this one to be too easy (evil laughter).

Begin with your hands on the dumbbells in the pushup position as shown. Execute a pushup and then using your midsection to hold everything tight, turn and pick up the dumbbell and extend it upward in the air forming a "T" position against the ground (se picture, this one is really hard to explain in words). Replace the bell to the ground and repeat with the other side. Each side counts as one rep (start each set on the arm opposite the arm you started the previous set with). Once you have knocked out five of these devilish bastards, perform five dumbbell burpees by jumping your feet between the bells, bringing them to your shoulders, and pressing them overhead.

Rip through ten sets of this monster and then go seek comfort somewhere warm.

Continued on next page…

#34 Front, Back, GO!

This is one holds a special place in my memory. This was a favorite conditioning and punishment tool used by various superiors at different points in my military career. The concept is simple. "Front" means pushups, "Back" means flutter kicks, lying flat on your back (hands under your butt is acceptable) and kicking your outstretched legs in an alternating fashion from a point roughly 6" off the ground, and "GO!" means run in place (high knees).

Setting this one up as a conditioning workout can be done a few ways. You can set a timer to beep at various intervals, signaling a fast transition to another movement, you can go of a stopwatch, changing at predetermined time hacks for a set period of time, or you can do it in it's best incarnation, as a partner assisted exercise with your partner calling the commands at random time intervals for a set period of time. I'll leave this one up to you.

I can still hear the sound of "On your belly, on your back, on your feet" being sung to the tune of "If you're happy and you know it" playing in my head thinking about my good times with this one.

#35 IMT, "I'm up, He sees me, I'm down!"

In keeping with our theme here after Front, Back, GO! I'll share another one that any of you military people will certainly have fond memories of I am sure. This one is the practice of "IMT", Individual Movement Techniques. This is accomplished by sprinting, getting down in the prone position, popping up, sprinting, and repeating the process ad nauseam. The intent here is covering ground on the enemy while minimizing your exposure to enemy fire. The mantra "I'm up, he sees me, I'm down" is played in your head during each of your efforts. The idea is to be back down in the prone before the enemy has time to effectively aim and fire at you.

I've used this one for years with clients. Females in particular love this one for some reason. In those cases I announce the trips to the prone with "GO!" or whistle blows. This one can easily be done with a little discipline on your own. Any terrain will work, though a few trips across a nice open field will leave you better conditioned than when you start and with a feeling of general badassness.

When you finish this one thank a Vet.

#36 400m Walking Lunge/ 400m Dash

Hit the track or your measured 400m-road course for this one. This is pretty straightforward, complete one lap around the track by walking lunge, keeping your torso as upright as possible and dropping (not slamming) your knee to touch the ground on each step, immediately followed by a balls out sprint lap. No need for more distance here. This doesn't sound like much, but it sure is nasty. Be honest on the walking lunges and leave nothing in the tank on the sprint. The urge to cruise, and take it easy on that lap will be high, fight it and make it the hardest quarter mile you've ever run.

You'll have nightmares about this one.

#37 Kettlebell Swing, Swing, Catch, Goblet Squat x 50

Fun stuff here. Grab a moderately heavy kettlebell and swing it to eye level. On the second swing, catch the bell in the goblet position as shown. Holding the bell in this position perform a squat. At the top of the squat, push the bell out and catch it, going into the swing to start the second rep of this ball buster.

Rip through 50 of these as fast you can. There is a certain rhythm to this one. It'll take a bit of practice to get the groove just right unless you are a born dancer like myself.

#38 5 Mountain Climbers + 1 Burpee x 25

Quick, nasty, and effective, this one will give you iron lungs for sure.

Bust out five mountain climbers, holding your body in the pushup position, and bringing your knees up to your chest or higher in an alternating fashion (as shown). One left plus one right equals one repetition. Upon completion of the fifth mountain climber, jump to your feet and then leave the ground, burpee style. From the jump, immediately hit the deck and begin on another set of mountain climbers. Five mountain climbers plus one burpee equals one set. Twenty-five is the task here.

If you're a stud, feeling ballsy, and only take a few minutes to knock this out, wait a minute or two and then repeat the process for a second set.

Yeah, I called you out.

#39 15 Dumbbell Snatches, 10 Overhead Walking Lunges Max Sets in 10 minutes

Set your countdown timer or start your stopwatch. Pick up a moderately heavy dumbbell (remember, it's too heavy if you can't keep moving with it and need to frequently set it down) and Snatch it 15 times with one arm. Upon completing the 15th rep, keep the bell locked out overhead and execute 10 walking lunge steps, counting each step as one. When you finish, switch hands and repeat. Do this as many times as possible in your ten minute window.

You'll certainly call me everything but a good guy for this one.

#40 Truck Pushes

Ok, this one is beyond simple. Distance, rest between trips, and number of trips will vary greatly based on your individual situation, but the gist here is to throw your truck (or car) in neutral and push the hell out of it.

That's all I have to say about that. Have fun with this one.

#41 Kettlebell Turkish Get-Up + 3 Snatches + 3 Overhead Squats, Max Reps in 7 minutes

You'll need a moderately weighted kettlebell for this one, though a dumbbell will also work. Begin by laying flat on your back with the bell extended out in front of you. Keeping the bell at arm's length, get to your feet with the bell pressed out overhead. Once you're there, knock out three snatches followed by three overhead squats. That represents one repetition. Set a seven-minute timer and bust out as many reps as you can before the buzzer, alternating sides each time.

Continued on next page…

#42 150 Jump Squats

Doesn't get any simpler than this. This one is for when you are seriously pressed for time, have no equipment, and just want to get something in for the day. This reminds one of my former stay at home mom clients who would have go-to conditioning workouts she could do based on how many minutes she had in between events with her young kids.

Squat to depth, come up, leave the ground by a few inches on each rep, repeat 150 times as fast as possible. That's it.

#43 10 yd Bear Crawl Shuttle, 40 yd Shuttle Max Reps in 5 minutes (2 rounds)

Hit the football field for this one. Begin on the goal line and bear crawl out to the 10 yd line and back. Once you get back to the goal line, turn and sprint out to the 40 yd line and back. The above represents one repetition. Set a five-minute clock and blast through as many of these as you can before you run out of time. Once you're through, take a two-minute break and get back at it for a second time.
Record your score and come back gunning for it another time.

#44 10 yd Dumbbell Bear Crawl, 10 Push-up/ Row x 6

Here's one that's deceptively nasty. Mark out a ten-yard course and get yourself two moderately weighted dumbbells (again, you want to be able to perform the movements without stopping because the bells are too heavy). Holding the dumbbells, bear crawl out to your mark and then bang out ten pushup/ rows, counting each row as a repetition (not one left plus one right equals one). Repeat five more times for a total of six sets.

Studs, if you're cruising on this one (much less than ten minutes) make the bells a bit heavier or add sets in groups of two.

#45 Descending Ladder from 9: Dumbbell Squat and Press/ Windshield Wiper

Get a pair of heavy-ish dumbbells. Pull up a spot near a chinning bar where you can execute your windshield wipers. Squat and Press the dumbbells for nine repetitions and then hop to the bar and perform nine windshield wipers (se photos for demonstration). Work your way down to one doing equal numbers of each movement. Make the reps high quality on the wipers, be honest with yourself. If these are out of your league at the moment, simulate the side-to-side motion of the windshield wiper at the top of a hanging knee raise.

Awful, just awful.

#46 100m Sandbag Waiters' Walk/ 35 Sandbag Squats x 4

Back on the bag for this one. Hoist it overhead and walk, arms extended for 100m. When you arrive at your mark, hold the bag in any manner you want and bust out 35 good squats. Turn around and repeat for a total of four trips.

Short and intense, keep it simple.

#47 400m Sandbag Waiters' Walk with 1 Sandbag Burpee Every Ten Steps

You'll need your sandbag for this one, and a 400m course or track. This is a ruthless smoker. You'll curse me for this.

Put the bag up overhead, waiter's carry style and start walking, counting each step. Every tenth step, drop the bag down from overhead and perform a sandbag burpee. Get the bag up overhead and get back on the move.

This one's all about time. Set a record, and just beat it, beat it.

#48 The "Gladiator-Maker" x 25

This one is a hybrid of the Gladiator Pushup and the Manmaker. These are legendarily brutal around here.

Execution is not as complex as it seems. Hold two dumbbells (you're going to need to take it easy on the weights on these, trust me), assume the pushup position, hands on the bells. Perform a row with the left arm as in the manmaker, then return the bell to the floor and perform a good pushup. After the pushup, turn to the side and extend the left bell up towards the sky as shown as in the Gladiator pushup. Replace the bell to the floor, bust out another pushup and then repeat the process with the right side (note: each rep will contain a total of three pushups). After you have completed the right side and replaced the bell to the starting position, jump your feet up, clean the bells to your shoulders, and press them overhead. That makes one repetition.

Tough it out through twenty five and call it a day. Gradually move to heavier bells when you can knock this one out in a few minutes.

Continued on next page…

#49 5 Dive Bombers/ 10 Mountain Climbers/ 5 Burpees x 7 sets

Hit the deck and complete 5 dive number pushups (as shown below). Once you're done, knock out 10 mountain climbers, counting one left plus one right as one single repetition. Upon finishing the last mountain climber, hit 5 burpees to complete the set.

7 of these bad boys, in a hurry is the task for today. Rip through them; just be sure to make the movements solid (particularly the dive bombers, don't skimp on these when the going gets tough).

Just a word of warning, don't do this one on a full stomach.

 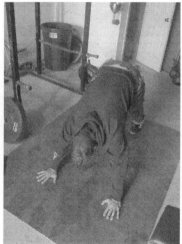

The Dive Bomber Push-up. Demo continued on next page…

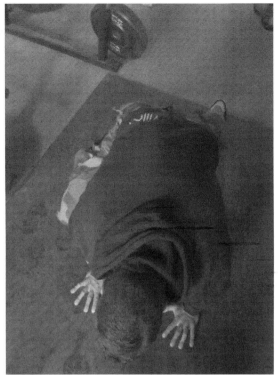

#50 The Sandbag Suicide Shuttle

Set up two markers, one at 20 yards, and one at 40 yards. Begin holding the sandbag at the starting line. Sprint to the 20yd marker and back, drop the sandbag off and sprint out to the 40yd marker and back. That completes one trip. Rest for 30 seconds to a minute and go again. Like the 100m repeat, this one is built up over time. Begin with 4 trips or so if your conditioning is not phenomenal. Build up to 8-10 trips over time, and track your progress in speed as well.

This is no joke.

#51 (Floor Wiper x 5, Bar Push-up x 10) x 6

Begin by loading a barbell to the desired weight. Big boys will probably use 135lbs as shown. Really the weight is not terribly important on this one, so don't stress it too much, 135 is just a good weight for most bigger, stronger, well-endowed guys. The hardest part, and limiting factor in selecting the weight is going to be getting it into position to start. This should be done by yourself, from the floor, not by using a rack or a partner.

Hold the bar at arms length over your chest while lying supine. Bring both of your legs up as in a leg raise, turning them to the side until your feet touch the plate on one side of the bar and then bring your feet to touch the plate on the other end of the bar. That completes one repetition of the floor wiper. Complete five reps and then transition to the bar pushup which is simply a pushup performed while gripping the bar as shown. All the way on these, body rigid, chest to the bar, no half-assing.

Knock out six sets of this ball buster, record your time, and call it a day.

#52 Sandbag 50/50 Mile

Awful.

This one is simple. Go to a track or other suitable one-mile course that features a quarter-mile loop. Haul ass around the first lap holding a sandbag. Upon completing the first lap, ditch the bag and run the second lap with just the weight of your own genitals encumbering you. Pick the bag back up for the third lap, and then nix it again for the fourth.

Vomit, sip water, record your time and go home proud.

#53 Double Dumbbell Turkish Get-Up x 25

Deceptively horrible.

Many of you reading this will have already done the Turkish get up. It is a great exercise and has a certain fun quality to it. These do not have that quality.

Select two equally-weighted dumbbells (you'll probably end up dropping down in weight, so be modest), one for each hand, lie supine on the ground with the bells at arm's length over your chest. Get up from the ground to a standing position with your arms extended overhead. Repeat for a total of twenty-five reps. Curse my mother for birthing me, and rest for tomorrow.

#54 Sandbag Burpee/ Burpee Descending Ladder from 10

This one really isn't that bad, really. Ok, I'm lying.

Simple and to the point, descending ladders are great. Start by knocking out ten sandbag burpees (as shown below). After completing ten of those beasts, bust out ten burpees without the sandbag. Once those are done do nine of each, then eight of each, and so on until you get to one and one.

The things we do to be better than everyone else…

#55 Kettlebell Sit-up, Swing, Goblet Squat 5/10/10 x 10

Grab a moderately weighted kettlebell for this one, no hero stuff.

Start by holding the KB on your chest and performing five good quality sit-ups (these will be the most challenging part of the workout if you use an adequately weighted bell). Stand up with the KB and knock out and perform ten swings. Catch the bell at the top of the last swing and perform ten deep, goblet squats to complete one set. Do nine more sets like the first one to make ten total and log your time to completion.

#56 50 Overhead Dumbbell Sit-ups, 800 meter dash

So simple, yet such a terribly despicable combination.

Here we feature our old go-to the overhead dumbbell sit-up. It's simple in design, hold two equally weighted dumbbells extended over your chest while lying on your back, and sit up. Your arms will be extended over your head as in a seated press at the top of the movement. You can anchor your feet, or leave them free for an even more exhilarating experience. Once you finish fifty of these gut-busters, take off on a half-mile sprint towards godliness.

Write down your time for today's conquest and hit the showers. Destroy your time on the next try.

#57 Burpee Broad Jump 400m

Another one for the track.

This one is beyond simple, but the farthest thing from easy. It will eat you for lunch.
You are simply going to execute one burpee broad jump (as shown) after another until you
make it one full lap around a 400m track. As always, record your time so that you can smash it
on the next go-around.

#58 Sandbag Clean and Press x 3, Overhead Squat x 3, Max Sets in 7 minutes

We don't need no stinking prowler.

Take your $5 sandbag that you built and get ready to manhandle (these sandbag drills get you ready for the husky jawns).

Bust out three clean and presses with the bag, touching it to the ground each time. Leave the bag overhead after the third press and knock out a trio of deep, overhead squats. That makes one set complete. Set a clock for seven minutes and do as many sets as you can in that time.

#59 50m Backward Crab Walk/ One Legged Push-up x 20, x 4

Grade school gym class with a military twist.

Mark out a fifty-meter course and assume the crab walk position at the start line. Crab walk backwards to the fifty-meter mark and execute twenty one leg push-ups (stick one of your legs straight up in the air boner style throughout the movement), switch extended legs with each repetition.

Four trips and fours sets of twenty push-ups and this one is over.

#60 Dive Bomber Push-up x 10, Mountain Climber x 10, 100m Sprint, x 4

This is one is a blast if you are a masochist.

Find a one hundred meter course (hit the track or mark one out) and assume the push-up position at the start line. Perform ten high-quality dive-bomber push-ups (as shown). Once you are finished the dive-bombers, stay in the push-up position and execute ten mountain climbers (pump your knees in an alternating fashion to meet your arms) counting left plus right as one repetition. Once you're done the two movements, break out of the push-up position into a balls-out sprint towards the finish line.

Rest at the finish until you are ready to hit it again. Record you times as heats, a separate time for each try.

#61 Situp x 10, Hanging Leg Raise x 5, Chin-up x 3, Max Sets in 10 minutes

Bodyweight and a chinning bar are that are needed for this one.

Bust ten sit-ups, then jump or climb to the bar and bring your legs up straight in front of your face. Control your body, do not swing around like an ass on the bar. Once the leg raises are complete, execute three solid chin-ups, bringing your throat to the bar and coming to full extension of the elbows at the bottom. This makes one set, do as many sets as you can in ten minutes and record the number to slay later like yesterday's ass.

#62 Dive Bomber Push-up x 10, Sandbag Squat & Press x 10, X 6

This one is a real bastard.

Get your trusty sandbag out for this one. Use the 80lb'er if you're of the abnormally hung variety.

Simple and to the point, ten dive bombers, then ten squat and presses with the sandbag makes one set. Do six of these beasts and record your time. Good luck.

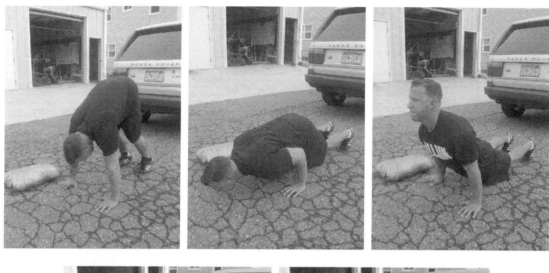

continued on next page…

#63 The Sandbag Mile

The bigger brother of the Sandbag half mile, it is as the name implies, one mile as fast as possible carrying a sandbag in any manner that you see fit.

Tons of fun. Have at it.

#64 Kettlebell Swing/ Burpee, 30 seconds/ 30 seconds for 7 minutes

Push this one out to ten minutes or two or three five-minute rounds when you're more of a beast.

Swing a moderately weighted kettlebell (we want lots of swings here) for thirty seconds, and then bust as many burpees as you can for thirty seconds immediately following the swings. Repeat this cycle for seven minutes. This will obviously require some sort of timer. I will let you figure out how to rig that one up. My job is to bring the pain.

#65 Sandbag Turkish Get-up + Sandbag Burpee x 2, Max sets in 5 minutes

Quick and brutal, add time to this one if you must or dare.

Perform a Turkish get-up by with the sandbag by lying on your back and placing the bag on your shoulder, then getting to your feet (I really don't care how pretty it is). Once you are standing, knock out two sandbag burpees. That makes one nasty, uncomfortable set. Do as many of these evil bastards as you can do in five minutes and make it count.

continued on next page…

#66 The 400m Heavy Swing Walk

This is deceptively shitty.

Get yourself a heavy kettlebell or dumbbell, we should be talking at least one hundred pounds here. Dangle it between your legs JP style and take ten steps forward, counting left plus right as one step. Once you cover ten steps, swing that big old thing like you mean it five times and then repeat the process until you cover four hundred meters.

#67 Burpee From Hell x 50

An evil spin on and old favorite.

The burpee, perhaps the most hated movement in this book, and the one that I seem to be most enamored with using to inflict lung searing pain on clients looking for unparalleled conditioning. Here is a nasty add on to the old chestnut.

The movement begins the same as the normal burpee, however instead of jumping in the air once you jump to your feet from the bottom position, you roll onto your back and bring your legs over your head to touch the ground as shown. From there you roll back to your feet and jump in the air to complete one repetition.

Bust fifty of these monsters in as little time as possible. Add reps as needed as your junk expands.

#68 Kettlebell Swing x 20, Greyskull Grinder x 5, x 10

Whew.

Get yourself a moderate kettlebell. You won't want a heavy one for this.

Knock out twenty swings with the bell and then transition to the chin-up bar to crank out five repetitions of the Greyskull Grinder (one dead hang chin-up followed by one hanging leg raise). Quality of movement on the Grinders is key, but turn up the heat on getting through this bad boy. The movement counts are titrated just right to make this one very evil.

Record a time and smash it when you revisit this nightmare.

#69 Walking Lunge Step x 20, Squat x 25, 50m Sandbag Sprint, x 4

Holy jello legs.

This one is just terrible. Get your sandbag and mark out a fifty-meter course. Perform twenty-five walking lunge steps (no sandbag) counting each step as one (L = 1, R = 2). Once those are out of the way, crank out twenty-five deep bodyweight squats. After the squats are through, pick up the sandbag and haul ass on a fifty-meter sprint with everything you have.

Repeat four times and then move all of the items you will need in your house to the first floor to avoid the stairs for a few days.

#70 (Clean and Press, Front Squat, Sots Press) 5 x 5

Load up a bar with a challenging but doable load (this will take a little feeling out). In my experience most will start out too heavy for this one and need to reduce the weight. That is fine; don't sacrifice quality of movement for weight here.

Clean the bar to the shoulders and then press or push press it overhead. Return the bar to the "rack" position and then execute a front squat, pausing in the bottom. While in the bottom of the squat, perform a Sots press by pressing the bar overhead to lockout and then returning it to the rack. Once the bar is back in the rack position, stand to complete the squat and the complex itself. That makes one repetition.

Hit five sets of five of this complex with a one-minute rest in between sets. Very gradually increase weight on this one.

continued on next page…

#71 Power Snatch x 10, 40yd Bear Crawl x 3 Sets

Yes I'm aware I'm mixing units of measure in this book, it's ok though, some of my best friends are yards.

Load up a bar with a stout weight (this should be tough, but not so heavy that you have to stop multiple times throughout the sets with the barbell). Mark out a twenty-yard mark as a turn around. Hit the power snatch for ten reps and then bear crawl your happy ass down to the turnaround point and back to finish one set. Two more and call it a day.

#72 Tuck Jump x 20, Hanging Leg Raise x 10, Mountain Climbers x 20 Max Sets in 7 minutes

Revisit your last meal.

Bust twenty tuck jumps (knees to chest, no donkey kick bullshit), then hit the chinning bar for ten good quality hanging leg raises (knee raises are ok, but you should be on leg raises by now). Once those are out of the way, drop and give me twenty mountain climbers, counting left plus right as one rep.

It's ok to hate me for this, I won't be mad.

#73 Sandbag Shouldering/ Sledgehammer Swing, 30 seconds Alternating, x 6

Get your sandbag, tire, and hammer out for this one.

Start a clock and shoulder the sandbag (bring the bag from ground to your shoulder in an alternating fashion, left then right) for thirty seconds. At the thirty-second mark transition to swinging the sledgehammer at the tire as hard as you can for another thirty seconds. Rest for one minute and then repeat for a total of six minutes. Have a partner record how many reps of each you do during each set if you have that capability. If not do the best honest mental count that you can and try not to have more than a five-rep difference between the first and last set.

#74 Burpee Suicides

This is just what it sounds like.

Hit the football field or another suitable spot. Mark out four points spaced about ten yards apart. Start at the first mark and sprint to the second. When you reach the second spot hit five burpees. Once the burpees are complete, sprint back to the start point, turn around and head to the next farthest point. Hit five more burpees at that spot and then sprint back to the start. Repeat the process for the last point that is marked and sprint back to the start.

Rest for a short time and hit it again. Start with four reps or so and then work your way up as you get more conditioned.

These suck, nuff said.

#75 Devil Lunge x 10, Kettlebell Swing x 20, x 6

The devil lunge, aptly named.

The devil lunge entails doing one lunge step then jumping from the bottom of the movement, and switching legs in mid air perform this evil exercise. You land in the bottom position of a lunge with the opposite leg in front. One repetition is complete when both legs have been in the forward position.

Do ten of these ball busters and then swing a heavy kettlebell twenty times. Five sets and call it a day.

#76 200m, Hang Power Snatch x 3, Overhead Walking Lunge x 10 steps

Get yourself a moderately weighted barbell; again we are not looking to have to set the thing down a lot during the workout. Power snatch the bar overhead three times, leaving it overhead at the top of the third snatch. Take ten walking lunge steps, counting each leg as one step and then repeat the process until you have covered two hundred meters.

Grueling to say the least.

#77 100yd Sandbag Throw, Bear Crawl, Sandbag Burpee

Pick up your pet sandbag and hit the football field for this one.

Begin in the end zone and chest pass the bag as far downfield as possible, then get on all fours and bear crawl to the landing site. Once you reach the bag, perform one sandbag burpee, and toss the bag out in front of you at the top.

Repeat the process until you make it into the other teams end zone.

#78 5 minutes, High Knees x 10, Burpee x 2

This is a quick and easy (no equipment) ball buster.

Set a timer for five minutes and start pumping out high knees (jog in place, bringing your knees high into your chest). One left plus one right makes one repetition. Once you've reached ten reps, bust out two burpees.

See how many sets you can knock out before the buzzer.

#79 Kettlebell Swing to Catch and Goblet Squat x 10, Turkish Getup x 5, x 5

More kettlebell fun.

Perform ten reps of the swing to catch and goblet squat, swing the bell to eye level, then once again, catching the bell in the goblet position on the chest and then knocking out a deep, solid goblet squat. Hit nine more of these bad boys and then hit the deck for five Turkish getups. Switch hands each rep.

Five sets of this and then lay then it's shower and cigar time for the day.

#80 Dumbbell One Arm Squat to Press x 10, One Arm Dumbbell Sit-up x 10, x 10

Never a fun one.

You only need one dumbbell for this one. Hold the bell in your left hand and knock out ten squat to presses (it's exactly what it sound like, squat, holding the bell in the "rack" position then come out of the bottom and press the bell overhead at the top). Once you're done with those, hit the deck and, while holding the bell in your left hand outstretched over your chest, knock out ten sit-ups. The bell will end up overhead locked out at the top of the sit-up. That makes one set. Switch hands each set for a total of ten sets.

You'll learn all about the anatomy of your abdominal wall in the days to follow.

#81 Descending Ladder from 10, Dive Bomber Push-ups, Windshield Wipers

I love this one personally.

I have an affinity for the dive bomber, always have. Do ten of these great push-ups and then hit the chinning bar. From a dead hang, lift your legs straight up so that your feet are touching or close to the bar. Tilt your legs to the left and then to the right as in a car's windshield wipers to make one repetition. Do ten of these and then hop back down to the ground. Begin the process again, this time doing nine of each. Repeat, losing one rep each time until you are doing one rep of each exercise. Keep a time for this one if you like and try to beat it next time.

#82 Dumbbell Overhead Walking Lunge + Press x 10, Dumbbell Sit-up x 10, x 7

Gotta love the versatility of dumbbells.

Hold two dumbbells overhead waiters walk style. Lunge forward with one leg and hold the bottom position, keeping your knee about one inch off of the ground. While in the bottom position, bring the bells down to your shoulders and press them back overhead in a controlled motion. Stand and lunge forward with the opposite leg, repeating the pressing process in the bottom. Each leg plus a press equals one repetition. Do ten reps and then transition to the dumbbell sit-up. Lie on your back with the bells pressed at arms length over your chest. Sit-up, allowing the bells to end up over your head at the top of the movement. Anchor your feet if you like.

Seven sets and that's that.

#83 Sandbag Push-up x 10, 50m Sandbag Sprint, Sandbag Sit-up x 10, x 7

No fun, none whatsoever.

Mark out a fifty-meter course and grab your sandbag. Start at one end and bust ten push-ups on the bag, breaking from the last rep directly into a balls out sprint to the other end. At the end, throw the bag on your shoulder or across your chest and knock out ten sit-ups (humbling to say the least). Roll over Bony style and start over with the pushups to begin the second set. Seven of these bad boys on the clock, have at it.

#84 Sledgehammer Swing/ Squat, Alternating 20 seconds on 10 seconds off

Ok, so those of you familiar with the Tabata method, think of this as an eight-minute Tabata, alternating exercises each round. Twenty seconds of sledgehammer swings on a tire followed by ten seconds of rest, followed by twenty seconds of squats, then ten seconds of rest; end minute one.

Got it? You got it. Record the total number of reps you do during each round and score the session by the lowest number of reps you got of each in any round.

#85 Typewriter Pull-up x 3, Goblet Squat x 10, x 6

This is for the beasts among us.

Typewriter pull-ups are hard for those who aren't featherweights, so these will be ballbusters for any modern Viking. Hang from the bar and pull-up as usual until your throat touches the bar. Once you're up there "slide" over to one hand, then over to the other one. Come back to the middle and return to a dead hang. Do three of these and then dismount the bar. Pick up a heavy kettlebell and bust ten goblet squats to bring an end to the first set.

Six total sets for the day.

#86 Flutter Kick x 20, Backwards Crab Walk 25 ft, Mountain Climber x 20, Sprint 50m, x 6

Yes, you read that right.

Ok, so mark out a fifty-meter course. Start at one end and hit twenty flutter kicks, (left plus right equals one rep) think six and thirty-six (inches that is, six inches form the ground, thirty-six inches from the ground). Once you're through with those, crab walk backwards out about twelve feet, turn around and head back to the start where you will do the twenty mountain climbers (left plus right equals one rep). Break from the mountain climbers into a sprint out to the fifty-meter mark.

Walk it back and repeat five times, HOOAH!

#87 Bar Push-up x 5, Clean and Press x 2. Max sets in 5 minutes

Simple and brutal.

Load a bar with a moderately beastly load. Assume the push-up position on the uncooperative bar and knock out five push-ups. Immediately after the fifth rep, jump to your feet and clean and press the bar twice to complete one set.

Transitions should be fast and frequent, fill the five minutes with sets and record your score.

#88 Gladiator Push-up x 10, Kettlebell Swing x 25, x 5

Love these Gladiator Push-ups.

Hit ten of these bad boys (see below) and then get to your feet and move to your kettlebell. Swing that bastard twenty-five times.

That makes one set. You've got four more after that. They'll suck, so make them count.

#89 100m Dash x 3, Burpee x 25, 100m Dash x 3

A burpee sandwich.

A twist on one of my favorite workouts, the one hundred meter repeat. Hit the track and bust your ass on a one hundred meter dash. Walk back to the start point and repeat two more times for a total of three sprints. You'll do three more, but before you do you'll have to do twenty-five burpees.

Three sprints, a bunch of burpees, three more sprints, sounds like fun .

Time everything and record for accountability purposes, or don't, it doesn't matter, you'll get the stimulus and be more conditioned either way.

#90 Push-up x 15, Chin-up x 5, Sledgehammer Swing x 10. Max Sets in 7 minutes.

Jello in the arms, gotta love it.

Start a ten-minute clock and begin knocking out push-ups. Do fifteen of them and then jump to the chinning bar for five chin-ups. After your throat touches the bar five times, drop and pick up the hammer and Ike Turner the tire for a ten piece. Do this whole thing as many times as you can in seven minutes.

You'll be more of a man at the end of this, I promise.

#91 Sandbag Burpee, Squat, Press, Squat and Press. Max sets in 7 minutes.

Another one of these seven-minute killers. Grab your bag and hit the dance floor, time to get sweaty.

Burpee once, then hold the bag at chest level and squat it. When you reach the top of the squat, press the bag overhead like a boss. After that do one squat AND press rep to complete one rep of the complex.

Nail as many of these sandy broads as you can in seven minutes and keep score for locker room talk.

continued on next page…

#92 Crab Walk 40 yds, Sit-up x 25, Squat x 25, x 4

Recess. Cookies and fruit punch at the end.

Crab walk it forty yards and then assume the position; the situp position that is. Twenty-five of them and then twenty-five squats. Do this four times, get a drink form the water fountain and get back to your desk. Miss Jacobs is reading us that horse story after recess again (it's late as I type this, forgive me).

#93 Dumbbell Overhead Squat x 10, Dumbbell Squat and Press x 10, Burpee x 10, x 5

Grab a pair, moderate ones, remember I don't need you putting these down a hundred times like a sissy. Put them overhead and squat them ten times. Once those are out of the way bust ten squat and presses. After that it's burpee time once again kids; ten this time. That's it for one set, you've got five to do.

Get to work. Time it, beat it, you know the deal by now.

#94 50m Sandbag Sprint, 50m Bear Crawl, 50m Sprint x 5

Ball buster in every sense of the word.

Hit your fifty-meter course with your sandbag, and get ready to lose lunch. Hoist the bag up on your shoulder and haul ass to the other end, ditch the bag and bear crawl it back to the start. Once you're back home at the start point get to your feet and sprint it back to the bag (it'll be at the opposite side from where you started). That completes one set. Repeat the process four more times for a total of five sets.

Just remember once you start this one that it will end and that it's only five sets. Give it everything; it'll be over soon.

#95 Handwalk Push-up x 25, Sandbag Squat x 50, x 3

Sophistication in simplicity.

Sandbag time once again. Lay it down on the ground in front of you and assume the push-up position with one hand on the bag and one hand on the ground as shown below. Execute a pushup and then "walk" your hands across the bag and into the opposite configuration before performing a push-up on that side. Count each push-up as one repetition and knock out twenty-five before standing with the bag and executing a set of fifty squats (hold the bag across your chest or on your shoulder).

Repeat for a total of three sets and record the time it took to completion.

  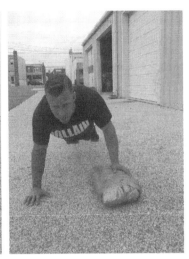

#96 Half Mile, 10 Seconds on/off Sprint/Bear Crawl

Hit the track again for this one.

Real simple, set a timer to go off every ten seconds or enlist the help of a partner (preferably a smokin' hot Viking groupie) to inform you when ten seconds has passed. Bear crawl as much distance as you can in ten seconds and then transition to a sprint for the next ten-second interval. Repeat until you've made your way around the track twice and then call it a day.

#97 Dumbbell Push-up/Row x 10, Mountain Climber x 20, Dumbbell Flutter Kick x 10, x 5

More sadistic dumbbell goodness.

Assume the push-up position on the pair of dumbbells (moderately weighted, the flutter kicks will keep you honest) and bust out a push-up followed by a row at the top. Count one repetition for each row (Left equals one, Right equals two). Do ten of these and then transition to mountain climbers for a twenty count, counting left plus right as one rep. After those are through, get on your back while holding the dumbbells with extended arms over your chest and pump out ten flutter kicks counting left plus right as one rep. That makes one set. Five of those are the mission for the day.

#98 5/5/5 Bar Push-up/ Hang Clean and Press/ Overhead Squat. Max Sets in 7 minutes.

This one is awful (not like any of them are not, but this one just blows).

Start a seven-minute clock and hit five good push-ups on your sandbag, followed by five hang clean and presses, followed by five overhead squats. One set down; how many will you do?

Clock's ticking.

That was lame, I know, but you can get away with the occasional lame write up when you're as handsome as I. I can always fall back on my looks to get me through life if need be.

#99 Power Snatch x 2, Overhead Squat x 2, Barbell Push-up x 2. 5 x 5.

Ok, so here's a fun complex.

Two reps of a power snatch with a stout but manageable weight, followed by two reps of overhead squat, followed by two push-ups on the bar. That's one repetition.

Five of these make a set. Do five sets of five, resting for a minute or more in between. Up the weight slow and steady on this one, it'll put hair on your chest that you can then enlist Bony to help you in waxing if that is your thing.

#100 100yd Bear Crawl with 10 Mountain Climbers at 10yd marks, Sprint back x 2

That looks confusing but is pretty simple actually.

Start at the goal line and bear crawl towards the away team's goal. Once you hit the ten-yard line bust out ten mountain climbers. Do the same at each ten-yard point on your way to the other end of the field. Once you reach the end zone, turn around and sprint it back like your life depends on it. Repeat the process one more time and then hit the locker room. Pants an underclassman and move somebody's clothes while they're in the shower. Just don't take anyone's iPod, that's a dick move.

Appendix A: How to Make a Sandbag

This Sandbag recipe is near and dear to me. When I started my business, these are what we used, seriously, these were all we had. Luckily things picked up over time and we have been able to add some tools since (earmuffs). Despite all of the wonderful new additions however, these sandbags remain great conditioning tools in our arsenal and are frequently used here by clients and made at home for their "homework". They will only cost you a few dollars to make and maintenance is too easy. When they get beat up, just drop them in another bag and wrap them with more tape. You've got nothing invested here, and they will more than pay for themselves in their positive effects on your training.

Step 1: Buy the Necessary Materials

You will need:

Contractor Bags

A 50 or 80lb bag of gravel or play sand (gravel is less messy).

Duct tape.

Step 2: Put the Bag of Gravel in a Contractor Bag

Step 3: Wrap the Bag of Gravel up in the Contractor Bag

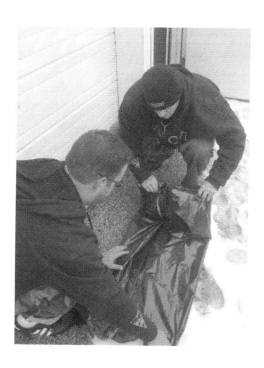

Step 4: Wrap the Hell out of it with Duct Tape to Complete Your Sandbag

The Finished Product in Use.
(Note Bony's sweet Yin Yang tattoo).

Your Author

John Sheaffer, aka Johnny Pain is the man behind the Philadelphia Pennsylvania area's infamous Greyskull Barbell Club. He is also the founder of Strengthvillain.com. He is the CEO of two corporations and is a proud father and slayer of gorgeous ass. He is available for consultations, live and online coaching, seminars, and speaking engagements.

John can be reached at:

john@villainintl.com

You can also follow JP on twitter:

@thejohnnypain

John also hosts a public Q&A forum on StrengthVillain.com where he entertains questions of all varieties, so make sure to stop over there and ask him any question you may have.

Special Thanks to my models:

Bony

Tommy Black and Grey

Smink

Made in the USA
Lexington, KY
05 December 2013